Rocky
Mountain
Adventures

Rocky Mountain Adventures

Betty Swinford

CF4·K

To my daughter Lynn

© Copyright 2004 Betty Swinford
ISBN: 978-1-85792-962-1
Reprinted 2010

Published by
Christian Focus Publications,
Geanies House, Fearn, Tain
Ross-shire, IV20 1TW, Scotland, Great Britain

Cover design by Alister Macinnes
Cover illustration by Graham Kennedy
Maps and other illustrations by Fred Apps

Printed and bound by MPG Books Ltd, Cornwall

Contents

Mountain Climbing

My husband, Bob, and I lived on a ranch in the Arizona desert. The name of the ranch was Rancho Vistoso. That means ranch with a view or a lookout.

Just across the road from the ranch were the stately but craggy Santa Catalina Mountains. In the winter months they were sometimes covered with snow, but during the summer they were ideal for hiking. Every night just after the sun went down the mountains took on a rosy glow. Then they didn't seem to have peaks and ravines at all. Instead they looked like they were made out of cardboard. That's how they got the nickname *Cardboard Mountains.*

The foothills leading up to the mountains were filled with wonderful and exciting things. At least to hikers like Bob and me. For instance, there were the crumbling remains of adobe (mud) walls where a Spanish mission had once stood. There were abandoned houses that still had things in them like brass beds, old sewing machines and gas refrigerators. Once we discovered an ancient windmill whose rusted vanes were struggling to turn in the hot desert wind. A trickle of red water dripped into a huge rusted tank below.

One day when Bob was free from ranch work, we took our bulldog and some food and set out to go mountain climbing. Like gigantic, rugged friends, the pinnacles of rock beckoned to us. However, to reach the mountains we first had to walk through a forest of Cholla (pronounced *choy-ah*) cactus. These cacti could be deadly. Their thorns could go right through your boots and into your feet if you even brushed against one. They grew with round joints that could be different lengths. Many joints fell to the ground, so a person took great care in not stepping on them.

We made it through the Cholla forest with only one mishap. That was when my foot touched a fallen joint and the thorns embedded themselves in my foot. It was very painful and I couldn't take a single step until Bob pulled out his pliers and removed it.

The way grew steep and rocky. I was in the lead with Bob and our dog behind me. Feeling perfectly safe now that we were away from the cactus, I wasn't paying much attention to where I was going.

Suddenly Bob yelled, "Betty, look out!"

He was too late. I heard a loud *hiss* beneath my foot and turned to see that I had come within a half inch of a deadly Gila monster! Its thick, forked tongue was flicking in and out. Its beady eyes never left my face.

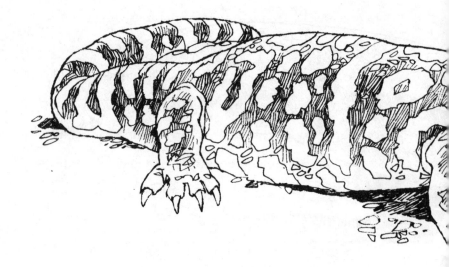

"Bob," I whispered, "it's beautiful!"

"It's also deadly. Back away from it slowly."

I learned later that there are only two venomous lizards in the world. One is the beaded lizard and the other is the Gila (pronounce *hee-lah*) monster. Orange and black, the Gila monster is beautiful and its skin looks beaded. A Gila monster grows nine to fourteen inches long. In the winter they hibernate. In the spring and summer months they search for bird or turtle eggs. They also feed off small animals, like baby rabbits. Their tongue is forked like a serpent's, but thick. When they

bite they hold on and chew, trying to get as much poison into their victim as possible.

Needless to say, I backed away from the lizard slowly. It had been a very close call and I'm sure that only the Lord protected me from being bitten.

We continued our climb, leaving the foothills behind and starting up the steep, rugged mountains. In places we had to pull our dog up by his collar. Then, at last, we reached a meadow lush with green grass and lofty pine trees. A cool mountain breeze was blowing. Bob made a small fire so we could cook hotdogs and make some instant coffee and we laid back against the grass to rest.

It was like entering a different world from the cruel hot desert with its many dangers.

I think about the traps and dangers Satan places before us. He will do anything to tempt us to lie, take something that doesn't belong to us or do other sinful things. That's why it's important to keep our eyes upon Jesus, just like Bob and I kept our eyes upon the heights of the mountains.

Maybe you remember Peter, one of Jesus' disciples. He got out of the boat to walk on the water to go to

Jesus. But he began to look at the storm instead of looking at Jesus and he began to sink. Jesus, in his faithfulness, reached out to Peter and saved him.

And the Lord shall deliver me from every evil work, and will preserve me unto his heavenly kingdom.
II Timothy 4:18.

Adopted Rabbits

The owner of Rancho Vistoso had a large German shepherd. We had a fourteen pound bulldog who *thought* he was a German shepherd! Now and then someone from the ranch would walk into the foothills and kill a jack rabbit so the dogs would have fresh meat. On this particular day, it was Bob's turn to kill a jack rabbit. Since I was an avid hunter myself, I went along.

Jack rabbits are native to the southwestern desert of my country. A grayish-brown in color, they are known for their great speed. They have long, powerful hind legs and very long, pointed ears.

A mother jack rabbit doesn't burrow into the ground and make nests to have her babies like cottontail rabbits do. Instead, she will choose a spot that she thinks is safe and have her babies there. The baby jacks are born with fur and with their eyes open.

They are vegetarians, and when the mother goes out to feed, she hides her babies. By calling to each other, she is able to find them again.

In Arizona, one never hunts rabbits during months that have an 'r' in them. That's when they get parasites. These could be dangerous to someone with a cut on his hand. They could get what is called 'rabbit fever'.

The sun was setting on this late afternoon when Bob and I walked into the foothills hunting for a rabbit. Since the hills were alive with jack rabbits, it didn't take long until we spotted one behind a tall cactus. Bob aimed his .410 shotgun and killed it with one shot.

When he picked it up by its long hind legs, he was astonished to see three newborn babies in a nest by the cactus! "Betty," he exclaimed, "this mother jack had just given birth!"

"Oh no" I cried, "they'll die without their mother!"

Bob sighed. "It's too late now." He stood there holding the dead rabbit and seemed to be deep in thought. Finally he murmured "I have an idea."

"What?" I asked, still feeling bad that we had killed a mother jack rabbit.

Gently he picked up the three tiny babies. "Let's take them home with us."

I was stunned. "Take them home?"

He shrugged. "They'll die anyway. Let's see if we can save them."

The idea seemed pretty wild, even to me. "You have to be kidding! How can we save them?"

"We'll feed them milk with an eye dropper." He handed me the baby jacks and we started for home. "It might work."

I began to catch his enthusiasm, and as soon as we got home we made them a little nest and began feeding them. Sadly, one of them died during that first night, but the other two looked like they might live.

To our amazement, our plucky little bull dog became more than just curious. He would lie down and let them

17

cuddle up against him. The baby jacks were sure he was their mother and we never told them differently.

Day by day the babies grew. Day and night our faithful dog cared for his strange adopted family. Then one night during a storm one of the rabbits got out of the house and disappeared. The other one, however, grew and thrived, content with its odd little 'mother'.

After a while we had to release the third rabbit back into the wild, but I got a good lesson out of this strange adoption. Here were two baby jack rabbits with nature's

completely different form Bo's, yet he gladly took them in as his family.

How like our Heavenly Father. We were born with sinful natures, totally different from God's nature. He is holy and perfect - sinless in fact. Yet when we accepted Jesus as our Savior, He took us in and adopted us into His family.

For we have not received the spirit of bondage again to fear; but we have received the Spirit of adoption, whereby we cry, Abba, Father. Romans 8:15.

Old Baldy

Bob and I made a trip into the Chiricahua (pronounced *Cheer-ah-cah-wah*) Mountains. It was November and that meant deer season had started. My husband and I hunted together every year and usually at least one of us got a deer to have butchered and placed in our freezer. Hunting was an important part of our life. It can go a long way to a feeding a growing family when you're struggling to make ends meet and living in a wild and rugged part of the country.

We parked our car in the rolling foothills. Donning red jackets so we could be seen by other hunters and carrying our rifles, we began climbing into the mountains.

"Have you got your deer tag?" Bob asked me.

I slung my rifle over my shoulder and patted my pocket, "right here."

Many people hunted the white-tailed deer illegally without tags. Some of them got caught and had to pay a huge fine.

"Let's head up that way," Bob suggested and pointed.

Straight ahead and far above us was Old Baldy. It was a gigantic mountain top of sheer rock that rose above all the other mountain peaks. People had dubbed it 'Old Baldy' because there wasn't a single tree on it. Getting anywhere close to it meant a long, hard walk. However, we were excited and eager to get higher where the deer were. Of course, I told myself, it was going to be a very long way back to our vehicle lugging a deer!

The cactus-covered foothills were soon behind us and we found ourselves in heavy trees. The ground beneath our feet was soft and springy with pine needles and dead leaves. Squirrels eyed us curiously, but mostly they were busy storing pine nuts and acorns for the winter ahead.

"It's getting awfully cloudy," I mentioned once and stopped long enough to get my breath and shift my rifle to my other shoulder.

Bob nodded, not as out of breath as I was. "We'd better stop talking. We're in whitetail country now."

No sooner had he said this than a deer broke brush just ahead of us. It had bounded out of sight before either of us could take aim at it.

It was cold, even though we were dressed warmly in boots and insulated parkas. An icy wind was blowing over the mountains. And was my vision becoming blurred? I couldn't see like I could an hour ago.

Still Bob plowed dead ahead, his red jacket to my wondering eyes turned pink. I stopped and

looked around. The trees were no longer green but gray. Then to my horror I saw that Old Baldy, our faithful landmark, was gone!

"Bob?"

He turned around to face me. He looked confused and concerned. "The clouds are coming down over the mountains," he said grimly.

The clouds thickened around us. We dared not take a single step for fear we might walk over a cliff. We could barely see each other. It was a complete whiteout, awesome and frightening. Without Old Baldy to guide us we had absolutely no idea how to get out of the mountains. We had lost all sense of direction.

"What are we going to do?" I asked and was surprised to hear myself whispering.

Deer hunting was forgotten. Bob stood there holding his 30-30 loosely in one hand. "We'll just have to wait it out."

We did just that. We sat down on the damp ground and waited. I knew, of course, that Old Baldy was still right there. Majestic and lofty as always, she was simply hiding from us.

The sun finally came out and burned away the clouds and we made it back to our car. But what an experience!

Do you ever feel like God is not listening to you when you pray? Are there times when you just don't feel

His presence? I've had times like that but God is still there just the same as ever. He hasn't disappeared. But there are times when He wants to see if we will believe in Him and trust Him when we can't feel anything. So for a little while He tests our faith.

Why standest thou afar off, O Lord? Why hidest thou thy face in times of trouble? Psalm 10:1.

Jesus said unto him, 'Thomas, because you have seen me, you have believed; blessed are they that have not seen, and yet have believed.' John 20:29.

A Lamb that Strayed

B ob had to make a business trip to Queen Creek, Arizona and he took his family along for the ride. Queen Creek was a dusty little town tucked away in the desert hills. An unpaved road led into the town at that time. There wasn't much there to see or do, but there was a good Mexican restaurant.

"Is Mexican food okay?" Bob asked us.

We all loved the hot, spicy food, so off we went to the restaurant for lunch. Bob ordered for all of us. Frijoles (beans – pronounced *free-holes*), tortillas (thin round bread baked on top of the stove) and cheese enchiladas (tortillas rolled into a tube and stuffed with cheese, then covered with a rich red sauce).

Our lunch over and Bob's business completed, we headed back through the dusty hills for home. The road wound like a serpent, and we were just rounding a curve that dipped down through a dry sandy waterway, when Bob slammed on the brakes. There to our startled eyes were at least 400 sheep making its slow, leisurely way across the road.

It took a very long time for the flock of sheep to make its way across the road and into the hills. The air was filled with their indignant and plaintive *baa*-ing. Not once did they look our way or appear to be concerned that we were waiting impatiently for them to pass.

Our girls, Lynn and Renee, were in the back seat of the car. Renee leaned forward to stare in disbelief at this unusual sight. "Mom," she asked curiously, "where's their shepherd?"

"Bob," I exclaimed, "she's right! Where *is* the shepherd?"

Bob was frowning and looking around. "I don't know, but a flock of sheep that big would not be wandering around out here alone."

At last, the final speck of wool walked past our car. Very slowly Bob moved on, just in case there were still other sheep that had not yet appeared.

"That seems to be all of them," I said aloud. "But I can't believe there's no shepherd!"

Bob shrugged. "Evidently this particular flock of sheep doesn't have one."

It didn't make sense. Unless the sheep had broken out of their enclosure and were on their own.

We drove on slowly, while Lynn and Renee were on their knees, looking out through the rear windshield for one last glimpse of the flock.

"Dad!" our daughter, Lynn, cried. "Stop the car!"

Bob pulled to the side of the road, thinking that Lynn had seen more sheep coming our way.

"Mom, Dad, look over there."

We all twisted around to see what our daughter was so excited about. There we saw a small lamb totally apart from the flock that was nibbling at a desert shrub. Standing behind the lamb and waiting patiently was our missing shepherd. He wasn't yelling at the small creature.

He didn't hit it. He was simply waiting for the animal to decide to go on.

One sheep, one little lamb, and the shepherd allowed it to wander. At the same time he never left it alone.

The Bible calls Jesus the Great Shepherd of the sheep. So many of us, at one time or, another, has wandered away from the Shepherd and the flock. But our kind and loving Shepherd has never forsaken us. His eye is always upon us as He waits and watches over us. He never walks on without us but lovingly woos us back to Himself.

If a man have an hundred sheep, and one of them be gone astray, does he not leave the ninety and nine and go into the mountains, and seek that which is gone astray? Matthew 18:12.

Meeting a Black Bear

Early on a Saturday morning our entire family drove back into the Chiricahua Mountains. Only this time it wasn't to hunt, it was to hike and explore. There were always so many caves and old mine shafts to discover and we were all nature lovers. However, we did have to watch where we were going, for some abandoned mine shafts went straight down into the ground. It was very easy for a person to fall into one of the yawning holes.

It was a warm, balmy day that grew much cooler as we climbed high into the mountains. We had packed our lunch and we were all eager to see what this day would hold. Little did we know that it would be an adventure none of us would ever forget!

"Dad," Renee asked excitedly, "will we see deer?"

Bob smiled. "Well, there are lots of whitetail deer in these mountains, so we could see some."

At the moment seeing some deer was the most exciting thing our children could think of.

In some parts of Arizona there are black walnut trees. We took time to gather a bag of nuts then we climbed higher into the mountains. When we finally reached a level spot, we began walking aimlessly through the trees. It really didn't seem like there was very much to get excited about, though we did discover an old, old tree house. After exploring what was left of that, we went on. We knew, of course, that there were bobcats, bears and even mountain lions in Arizona, but all we saw were some chattering, scolding squirrels playing around a tree and a few raccoons.

I think it was Lynn who saw the tall, wide board set into the side of a hill. "Mom, what is that?"

I turned around and stopped. "I don't know".

We went forward furtively and Bob wrenched away the board. A rush of cold, damp air hit us in the face, along with some familiar odor.

"Will you look at that!" Bob exclaimed in surprise.

There, against the wall of this old mine were a pick and shovel. The familiar smell had come from a big slab of bacon hanging to one side. Other food supplies, flour, sugar, coffee and pinto beans, were there too.

"Dad," our son Stephen cried in wonder, "it's an old abandoned mine!"

Bob shook his head and corrected, "Not so abandoned. Some prospector is trying to coax some more gold out of this old mine."

"Does he live in there?" Lynn asked. Her blue eyes were large with wonder.

"He could, I suppose. I see a pile of blankets over there."

There was a big smoke-blackened coffee pot and skillet over by the food supplies. Even though we knew that prospectors were rugged men and used to roughing it, we had a hard time believing that one actually lived in the old mine.

"Can we explore it?" Stephen asked hopefully.

"No," my husband told him. "We'd be intruding. Just put the board back and forget about it."

This was disappointing, but if we thought our adventures that day were over, we were sadly mistaken.

We continued to wander through the thickly wooded area. Birds flitted overhead. A half dozen raccoons played a game of tag. It was all wild and wonderful and we loved every minute of it.

Lynn touched my arm. "Mom, look! An old abandoned house. I *know* we can explore *that!*"

The house was a tumbledown thing that had not been lived in for years. Made of wood, its door sagged on rusty hinges. The window panes had been broken out and the roof looked like it was half gone. Just then Bob called out.

"Betty, Kids?" Bob's voice was low and very serious. "I want you to get inside that old house *right now.*"

I looked at him sharply. "Why? What's wrong?"

Grimly he whispered, "Just get inside, *NOW!*"

Lynn saw it before the rest of us. A big black bear was facing us. It wasn't at all far from where we were and it did not look happy about our being in its territory!

We didn't ask any more questions. We flew into that old house, wondering if it would come in after us.

It could, of course. There was absolutely noting to stop it. And if we made a break for it and climbed trees, that wouldn't solve anything. Bears, too, could climb trees.

We stumbled through all the rubble on the floor and went to stand by a window. The bear lumbered toward us, until it was right outside the window looking back at us. Its eyes never left us. If we ever needed the Lord's protection it was now.

We knew how dangerous black bears were. Every year campers were clawed badly as bears invaded their tents while they slept.

We watched, numb and horrified, as the great animal paced back and forth in front of us. It seemed to be

trying to decide whether to come inside the house and attack or move on.

Suddenly the animal seemed to sigh – probably my imagination – and turned around. With a last look our way, it disappeared into the trees.

The situation had been very serious and could have been deadly, but God was faithful and took care of us. He had even provided us with a tumbledown shack where we could take refuge.

Any time we are afraid or in danger, we can speak the name of Jesus and He will take away our fears and keep us safe. He will be our refuge in times of trouble and fear.

The name of the Lord is a strong tower; the righteous run into it and are safe. Proverbs 18:10.

My Narrow Escape

Our entire family loved to ride horse back. My daughter Renee even rode in front of me in the saddle before she was two years old. When I was fifteen years old I owned a beautiful white Arabian stallion. His name was Rocky and he taught me a lot about horseback riding. However, it was often Rocky's delight to let me ride about five miles from town, then rear onto his hind legs and charge back to his pasture. He spooked easily and would lunge sideways at the smallest shadow.

In fact, if you live in certain parts of the Rocky Mountains it is essential to have a horse, and to be able to ride it well. The horse in this story was named Lady and she was a sweet little brown mare, calm and even-tempered.

Bob and I had made reservations to go to the little town of Patagonia for an overnight stay and a ride into the Huachuca Mountains the following morning on horseback. We had left our children with a sitter and set out alone for our great adventure.

Patagonia was a very small town in southern Arizona. There wasn't much there, but there was a good Mexican restaurant.

"I can't believe it's just the two of us," Bob grinned.

"But we need to call home from the restaurant and make sure everything is all right," I told him.

We settled into the rustic cabin we had rented, headed for the restaurant and called home. Everything was fine. We ate, returned to the cabin and waited impatiently for morning to come.

We left Patagonia very early. The day was cool and pleasant and our ride would be a long one. It would be dark by the time we came back.

There were about twenty of us in the group. Three of the men were guides and the rest of us were tourists. We were just a happy, carefree bunch of people, out for a wonderful ride. I thought!

We rode through a bubbling stream and started up a trail into the mountains. The horses were frisky and wanted to gallop, but the trail grew narrow and twisting and the guides told us to hold them in. I was riding Lady, and she really behaved like a lady.

As we climbed higher and higher, a sheer cliff appeared on our right. The trail was so narrow that we had to ride single file. Looking down hundreds of feet, we could see a clear, meandering stream of water. There were houses and other small building here and there. They were lonely-looking structures tucked away in these rugged mountains.

We entered towering pine trees, and after a three hour ride we suddenly came out on a clearing big enough to eat and rest before starting for home. Tired, hungry and thirsty, we dismounted and milled around talking. The guides busied themselves making a fire and heating food. Bob and I stood with several others at the edge of a cliff and looked away into space. The air was clear as crystal and you could see for miles.

One of the men nearby pointed. "If you look away over there, you're actually looking into old Mexico."

Bob was stunned. "Mexico? No kidding?"

"Yes, our new friend replied. "That's because the air here is so pure. Do you know how far it is to Mexico?"

Bob shrugged, "Forty miles?"

The man nodded, "at least."

Behind us, one of the guides was making cowboy coffee in an ancient blackened coffee pot. He explained that you get the water boiling, and then throw in a handful of coffee grounds. After that you toss in a cup of cold water and that makes the grounds settle to the bottom. "Best coffee you'll ever drink," he promised.

It *was* great coffee! We drank it and ate the cornbread and beans they had brought for lunch. Then we settled back on blankets to rest before starting back down the mountain.

"Okay, folks," one of the guides told us after a while, "we have a long ride ahead of us. It will be dark by the time we get back to the stables so we have to get going."

We saddled up and were about to head back down that narrow trail along the cliff, when Lady suddenly

went crazy! She bolted forward, bucking and kicking, and started forward in a dead gallop.

I considered myself an expert rider, but Lady took me completely by surprise. It seemed like I forgot everything I knew about riding. Should I give her, her head, or should I pull back sharply on the reins? Then to my horror, I saw that she was racing headlong toward the cliff! If she went over it would be the end of my life. And I had three young children at home who expected me to return to them!

"Get her head!" one of the guides screamed.

Stunned and horrified, the others stood in silence, watching my out of control mare. Mere feet from the

edge of the cliff, I began thinking clearly again. Scooping up the reins, I pulled back hard and twisted her head to one side. We stopped about a foot from the drop-off.

Trembling and terrified, I dismounted and collapsed against my husband's shoulder.

"Everyone dismount" a guide ordered sharply. "We're going to take another hour to rest and try to find out what's wrong with that horse."

It took no time at all to find the problem. A small, sharp pine cone was under my saddle blanket. As soon as I put my weight on Lady, the cone cut into her back.

Only the Lord had saved me from going over that cliff. Did you know that God's angels watch over you? That means that nothing can happen to you as you live for Jesus unless God allows it. Perhaps when we get to heaven we will be surprised when we find out the many times our Lord has saved us from being hurt.

For He shall give His angels charge over you, to keep you in all your ways. Psalm 91:11.

A Mountain Shepherd

I would like to share a story with you I heard some years ago. It's about a shepherd named George and his favorite sheep named Lily.

'George lived in the High Country. The mountains of northern Arizona rise many thousands of feet and are always called the High Country. George was a wiry little man and getting old. His face was dark from wind and weather and looked like wrinkled leather. He stayed with his flock all year around and lived far from any town in a shepherd's wagon.

A shepherd's wagon was made of wood and wasn't very big at all. In a way it looked like a travel trailer, except that a shepherd's wagon was made for rugged living and was pulled by a horse. Inside was a narrow bed, storage space, a tiny stove for cooking and heat, his shearing tools and his food supplies. His life was rugged and lonely. At night he sat by a small campfire with his horse, his dog, Lily and the stars for company.

George loved his sheep, but his favorite was an ewe named Lily. She was as dear to him as his faithful dog or his horse. When Lily saw him coming, she would run

to meet him and baa happily. The two had an especially close relationship.

George was too far from civilization to have electricity or running water. So when shearing time came around he had to use old-fashioned hand clippers to shear his sheep. And now it was once again shearing time. He brought the sheep into an enclosure in order to control them. Then one by one he clipped away the wool. All during the shearing the sheep cried in terror.

As I have told you, George was an old man. His hands were gnarled with arthritis, and as he worked his hands

began to tremble. Always, he saved Lily until the last, and now he went to get her to clip away her wool. Lily gazed up at him with trusting eyes and did not once resist as the clipping began.

Before the shepherd had finished clipping her, his hands shook so badly that be nicked her skin. Still Lily stood in obedience while George finished the clipping even though he had cut her. George gathered up the wool while Lily stood a little apart from him, in pain. George knew he had hurt her and he sniffed and wiped his eyes. Then he reached toward Lily with cupped hands. Gently he whispered her name. *"Lily."*

Lily went to him at once and laid her soft face in his cupped hands. Lily gazed at her shepherd with love and trust, and George laid his face against the wooly head. They stayed that way for a long time. Lily had been hurt this way before and she knew she might be again. She also knew that her shepherd loved her and would never hurt her on purpose. She trusted him completely.

The shepherd always saved Lily until the last for he knew that his hands would be unsteady then. You see, George also trusted Lily. Even though she might be hurt in the shearing process, he knew she would never rebel

against him. It was a two-way relationship of complete love and trust.

The Bible says that we are God's sheep. Sometimes things happen in life that hurt us. Sometimes our hearts are broken. And there are times when God allows us to be hurt in some way. Not because He is weak and old like George the Shepherd, God is all powerful. It isn't because He likes to see us wounded either, but it is because God knows He can trust us. He wants us to trust Him just as Lily trusted her shepherd, knowing that our Shepherd will never hurt us on purpose either.

For He maketh sore, and bindeth up; He woundeth and His hands make whole. Job 5:18.

He healeth up the broken in heart, and bindeth up their wounds. Psalm 147:3.

A Foolish Mistake

Bob and I moved to Rancho Vistoso just after World War II. Jobs were very hard to find, so when Bob was offered a job on a real working ranch, he jumped at it. Besides living on a ranch was for us a dream come true.

He only earned a few dollars each month, but we were given a pretty little pink adobe house to live in and all our utilities were paid. We had no children at that time, so if we were careful we could get by all right.

In our front yard were a number of orange and grape-fruit trees. We could go out almost any time and pick our own oranges and grapefruit. In the spring the smell of the blossoms was so strong it was almost overpowering. Bob and I often went outdoors at night to enjoy the fragrance. The stars hung so bright they seemed close enough to reach up and pluck them from the sky. Coyotes howled all around the ranch. These were enchanted nights that I have never forgotten.

On this particular night when we went outside, Bob spied something wiggling through the grass. The only light came from the corral, so in the dark the thing was slender and looked to be about fourteen inches long, with black and white rings around its body.

Bob began to get excited. "It's a king snake! Betty, go get an empty jar and we'll catch it!"

Why he wanted to capture a snake I had no idea. I still don't. But being young and foolish, I rushed into the house and got an empty jar with a lid.

We both stooped down, intent on catching this beautiful king snake.

"Look out!" Bob yelled. "Don't let it get away!"

Long and loud, I protested, "But I don't *like* snakes!"

"Come on, it'll be fun. We'll show it to Tom (the ranch owner) in the morning and let it go."

I was all in favor of letting it go right then! We had found rattlesnakes around our yard a number of times. However, in the near darkness this one did appear to be very pretty. I kept asking, "Will it bite?"

Bob shrugged. "King snakes aren't poisonous."

I frowned. "I still don't want it to bite me."

It took at least fifteen minutes to capture the little snake. We'd almost succeed in getting it inside the jar when it would break free and try to wiggle away. Bob would place the open end of the jar in front of it so it would crawl inside, but it wasn't cooperating at all. Many times that night it nearly bit us. But at long last we got it in the jar and screwed on the lid.

Imagine our horror the next morning when we discovered that our innocent little king snake was actually a very deadly coral snake! The rings around its body weren't black and white at all they were black, yellow and red. In the dark we hadn't been able to tell the difference. We had done a very foolish thing in capturing that small snake.

Coral snakes are extremely poisonous. They usually grow to about 18 to 21 inches in length but can grow even longer. It's the only poisonous snake in North America that lays eggs. Living away out of town on a ranch, that snake's bite would have killed us!

People often do foolish things. Children play with matches and are often badly burned. That, too, is very foolish. We get only a small amount of rain in Arizona except during the monsoon season. Then all the dry streams and river beds are flooded with angry, swirling water. Every year people are swept away, foolishly thinking they can cross the raging rivers.

In the 13th chapter of I Kings we read a story about a prophet of God. God instructed the prophet not to stop at anyone's house and not to eat or drink with anyone on his way home. But the prophet paid no attention to what the Lord said and stopped at a man's house to eat with him anyway. Because of his foolishness, he was killed by a lion on his way home.

It's important to be wise and to ask God if what we are planning to do is right. Otherwise we can get into a lot of trouble.

If you want to know what God wants you to do, ask Him, and He will gladly tell you. James 1:5 (Living Bible).

Red Rock Crossing

Our summer vacations took us many places. Sometimes we went to California, where we visited Disneyland, Knotts Berry Farm and the Pacific Ocean. Twice we flew to Hawaii. But no matter where we went, nine times out of ten we ended up in Arizona at Red Rock Crossing.

The small town of Sedona is nestled in rugged, red Oak Creek Canyon. A 22 mile narrow road leads through the canyon and upwards to the High Country. Sedona is a tourist town, with many motels, restaurants, curio shops and art galleries. Oak Creek Canyon is a beautiful, majestic place formed from red sandstone. Surely it is one of God's masterpieces of creation.

Red Rock Crossing lies west of town, with rapidly running Oak Creek flowing all the way through it. Campers are not allowed at the stream now, but when our children were younger it was our all-time favorite place to park our camping trailer and end our vacation.

Big cottonwood trees kept the area cool, and once in a while we could see fireflies at night. Fireflies are things you almost never see in Arizona. There were hiking trails, swimming, fishing and tubing. There was even a long slippery rock you could slide down into a deep pool of water. Each camping trailer or tent had its own iron grill for outdoor cooking.

"Mom," Lynn told me one morning, "Renee and I are going to tube down the creek."

I cautioned her, "Don't go too far."

The last thing I heard from them was their giggling and whooping as they rode inner tubes down the swiftly moving stream.

"Don't you just love this, Lynn?" Renee crooned. "It's even better then playing in the ocean."

Lynn lay back in her tube, grinning from ear to ear. She felt like a butterfly just released from its cocoon. Their cutoff jeans were soaked, but who cared! This felt cool, free and wonderful.

"We're getting pretty far away," Lynn reported once. "Remember we have to walk back."

Renee waved an arm in the air. "I know, but so what!"

Suddenly the water grew shallow and their tubes bumped to a stop. Disappointed, they left the creek and started walking back on the dusty road. The water was too swift and there were too many rocks to try and wade back.

It was a hot day and the road was covered with burning hot river silt. After a dozen steps they knew they were in trouble.

"What are we going to do, Lynn? My feet are burning up!"

Lynn hopped from one foot to the other. "Renee, we're at least three miles from camp."

"But we'll never make it!"

Already their feet felt blistered. They tried racing from the shade of some shrub to the shade of a rock, but between the little bit of shade they found, the river silt was scorching the bottoms of their feet. In desperation they stopped and sat down on their inner tubes. However, they too were burning hot and they had to stand again.

"Jesus," Lynn prayed in despair, "Help us to know what to do!"

"Remember that time," Renee moaned, "when I found that horse running around loose and I got on it and rode it back to camp? I sure wish that horse was around now."

Lynn pointed. "Look. There's a farmhouse. Let's go see if someone will drive us back to Red Rock Crossing."

To reach the farmhouse, they had to cross a pasture filled with cows. Praying there wasn't a bull to charge them they made their way carefully to the door of the house and knocked, and knocked, and knocked. There was no one home.

They started out on the dusty road again. Their feet were red and becoming badly blistered.

Renee was about to cry. "I can't do this!"

Suddenly Lynn stopped and gasped. She had asked Jesus to show them what to do - he had answered by giving Lynn a brilliant idea. Quickly she tore off the back pockets of her denim shorts. Then she ripped out the front pockets.

"Here, stand on these," and Lynn handed her sister two of the pockets.

Next she tore loose threads from the bottom of her cutoffs and they tied the pockets to the bottoms of their feet! Stumbling and hobbling along, they made it back to camp hours later without further burning the soles of their feet.

God will always have an answer to our problems if we will only take the time to ask him what to do.

He will keep the feet of his saints… I Samuel 2:9.

The Sand Painting

Let's begin this story by going to the vast Navajo (pronounced *Nav-ah-ho*) Indian Reservation. It lies just a few miles from where I now live, and it's like entering another world. Some Navajos are Christians, but most are not. Their culture has been passed down from one family to the next and it is not only powerful, it can be very evil.

The older women wear tiered velvet skirts and turquoise necklaces. Older men wear their hair long and tied into a cloth at the back of their heads. They wear boots, denim pants and wide-brimmed hats.

When the men meet together for tribal meetings, they often use a kind of cactus called peyote. This causes them to have visions that are not from God but are supposed to give them guidance to make decisions.

Most Navajos still live in eight-sided houses called Hogans, with the door facing east. That's because they believe that Jesus will come from the east, even though they aren't Christians. Women crouch under a thatch roof shelter called a Ramada and cook blue corn tortillas over a small fire. Bright red chilies hang on the eaves of their Hogans to dry. They weave beautiful rugs and make jewelry out of silver and turquoise. They also make Kachina dolls, but most Christians will not have one in their homes because they are believed to be evil.

Slim, towering sandstone spires rise from the desert and seem to reach for the sky. In a place called Monument Valley there are many red rock formations that have stood in awesome stillness for centuries.

Witch doctors and medicine men still have great power over their people. Theirs is a pagan and unhappy way of life, and many of them are alcoholics.

One day a missionary was walking through Monument Valley, and saw a medicine man on his knees by a sand painting. He was chanting and waving feathers over it. A group of people stood around watching, so the missionary joined them. What he saw was a small girl lying on the sand painting. She had tuberculosis and the medicine man was trying to cure her.

The medicine man would take sand that had been dyed different colors and make a design on the ground. Then the sick person would lie down on the design and the medicine

man would perform a ceremony to try and heal them. But of course only God can heal! When the sick person was ready to die, they often left them alone with water and something to eat, (food to take with them into the next life). If only the Navajos had known they could pray!

This is a story that made my heart feel sad. You see, when my precious daughter Lynn was eight years old she had cancer of the brain. It could not be operated on and the doctors said she would live only six to twelve months. Never have I prayed so hard! Many, many other

Christians were also praying. The day before her surgery, our pastor and some men from the church went to the hospital to pray for Lynn.

The day of her surgery was the hardest day of my life! We waited for four long hours. Then a surgeon burst through the door looking utterly bewildered. "We know it's there," he told us. "We just can't find it."

They had hoped to get a smear of the cancer to see if it would respond to cobalt treatments and prolong her life a little but the cancer had disappeared.God had answered our prayers with healing. How different it might have been for that little Navajo girl if her people had known Jesus. However, sometimes Jesus does not choose to heal; other times He does. The Bible says 'that in all things God works for the good of those who love him,' Romans 8:28. God is able to turn any situation around. We must pray to him. Lynn left the hospital a healthy little girl. Her hair grew back and she returned to school. The cancer never came back.

And this is the confidence that we have in Him, that if we ask anything according to His will, He hears us; and if we know that He hears us, we know that we have the petitions that we desire of Him. I John 5: 14, 15.

Cheese and Crackers

It was November and it was Thanksgiving Day. The owner of Rancho Vistoso had sold the ranch and the new owner moved his household servants into our pretty little adobe house. Not knowing what to do with us, he moved us into an old unused tin laundry room.

We were crushed. During the monsoon season, Bob had tried to drive through a flooded *arroyo* (a stream bed) and lost the engine to our old Dodge. It seemed like everything we had had been taken from us. Thankfully we had no children at that time.

It was very cold and heavy clouds said it might snow. Our new 'home' was bitterly cold, though there were two ancient stoves in it. One was a strange old kerosene one, and the other was a tiny cast iron stove for heating. But it was still impossible to heat the place. At night we could lie in bed and see the stars through the tin roof. The small amount of money we had, had to be spent on blankets, and all we had to eat for lunch that day was cheese and crackers.

It was a very bleak time. We were brand new Christians and our faith was being tested. Still, I don't think we ever missed a church service. Somehow we always managed to get a ride into Tucson and then some kind Christian would drive us back home. But that day we couldn't bear to be cooped up in that tin room, so we took a long walk down *Caò del Oro*. That's Spanish for Cañon of Gold. It was a wide sandy river that only had water in it after a hard rain. Then men would come and pan for gold. Many nuggets were found that way. That's how the river got its name.

A few snowflakes began to fall and we hugged our jackets tightly around us. Now Bob and I had run into bobcats, mountain lions and bears in Arizona, but we had never seen a black panther. In fact, black panthers were never seen in Arizona! That was about to change.

We had been talking about God's promises. I had begun memorizing scripture verses as soon as I accepted Jesus as my Savior, and now I quoted softly, "'but my God shall supply all your needs according to His riches in glory by Christ Jesus.'" (Philippians 4:19)

"Yeah," Bob sighed, "Things will get better. It won't always be this way." He laughed softly and said wryly, "I can't imagine sitting down to turkey and cranberry sauce like other people are doing today."

"But we have Jesus," I reminded him, "and if I had to choose between all that wonderful food and knowing Jesus, I'd take Jesus any time."

He squeezed my hand and suddenly tensed. "Look up there on the river bank."

In a low crouch, staring at us through slitted eyes was a huge black panther! It sat there crouched on its belly watching us.

"I didn't know there were black panthers in Arizona," I said in a hushed voice.

"There aren't. It had to have come across the border from Mexico."

It was a beautiful creature and for a long time neither of us moved. The only gun Bob had brought was a .22 rifle. Lifting it, he fired a shot into the air. The big cat jumped in alarm. A second later it was running away.

We stood there with thundering hearts. Oddly enough, seeing that panther, and spending time talking about God's faithfulness had brightened our day. We went home and Bob started a fire in the stove. We huddled around it, gave God thanks for our cheese and crackers, and ate. And we were truly thankful!

In school we have tests to see how much we're learning. God gives us tests too see if we can pass them. Small ones and big ones. Let's be thankful, no matter what tests He gives us.

The Apostle Paul said... *"I have learned how to get along happily whether I have much or little. I know how to live on almost nothing or with everything…whether it be a full stomach or hunger, plenty or want…" Philippians 4:12 (Living Bible).*

Beautiful but Deadly

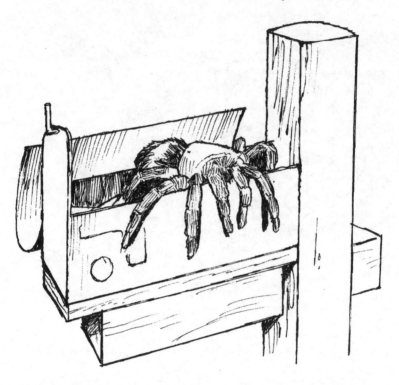

The desert is an interesting place and full of surprises. Some are only curious. Some are beautiful. Some are deadly. Everything however is created by our great God. Even spiders!

One morning I walked down the long lane to the mailbox. To my horror, I opened the lid and a huge hairy spider leaped out and onto my arm! It was a tarantula, the largest spider in the world. They're covered with brown hair and have eight legs.

While tarantulas inject venom into insects and small lizards, their bite to a human causes only itching and a little painful swelling. For the fear it put in my heart it may as well have been deadly.

A tarantula's home is hard to find. They either burrow into the ground or live in trees. They grow to be at least the size of a man's hand, and many people may even keep them as pets.

Another desert creature that really *is* poisonous is the scorpion. There are about 1,300 different kinds of scorpions and are believed to be relatives of mites, ticks and spiders. Their bodies are long and their tail is a separate segment with a vicious stinger at its tip. They usually have a pair of eyes in the front and two to five more pairs on the sides. Though they are often found in sandy deserts, they love cool, damp places like tubs and showers.

If you live on the desert you learn to shake out your shoes each morning before putting them on, for scorpions like to nest in shoes during the night.

I have two friends who were hospitalized from scorpion stings. There was pain; swelling and even for a short time they were paralyzed. Arizona desert scorpions are usually not very big, though some species grow to a great size.

So you have to be careful in the Rockies with all the little creatures and plants around that could bite you or hurt you - or even kill you. But some things can actually save you - and are therefore very useful indeed. Let me tell you about two kinds of cactus that have actually saved men lost in the desert.

One is the mighty saguaro (pronounced, *sa-wa-ro*) cactus. The saguaro grows to a great height and has thorn-covered arms that grow upwards. Their inner framework is woody spines and people used to make lamps and furniture from them. Their thorns are thick and curved like fishhooks.

People who have become lost on the desert pierce the saguaro and water flows out for them to drink. They also grow a kind of large berry on top that Indian women used to pick with a long pole and make jam.

Another cactus plant that has saved lives is the prickly pear or 'paddle' cactus. Its nicknamed the paddle cactus because it looks like it's made up of paddles. Sometimes the only thing in the desert to eat is the paddle cactus. You simply cut off one of the paddles and roast it over a fire. They taste something like okra. The paddle cactus has other uses too. Rich red fruit grows around the edges of the paddles and make the best jam you will ever eat. I used to pick them by spearing the fruit with a screw driver, placing it in an old pillow case and boiling it. This

protects you from the thorns and boiling makes it easy to take off the skins.

Then there's the mesquite tree. It's a thorny tree that bears long, hard bean pods. Indian women used to pick them, put the beans in a stone bowl and pound them with a pestle into flour for baking.

Another beauty in the desert during the spring months – besides the flowering cacti – is the many wild flowers that cover the desert and rolling hills.

You can drive for miles and the ground will be solid with wild flowers. Photographers spend hours taking pictures of the beautiful landscape.

So now you know some more about the Cactus plants. Perhaps you thought they were just akward thorny plants before - not much use for anything. Well, now you know better. What a wonderful, beautiful world God has given us to enjoy!

For by Him were all things created, that are in heaven, and that are in earth. Colossians 1:16.

An Arizona Christmas

B ob and I left ranch life for a small three-bedroomed home in Tucson, Arizona. It was, however, the roughest year of our lives. For the third time in my life I was sick with tuberculosis. Our children weren't well and doctors said that our daughter, Lynn, would die within the year. There were medical bills to pay and Bob didn't make much money so with Christmas on the way, there was no money for gifts. None!

Just before Christmas the doctors said I was well again and Lynn's cancer was completely gone! We had a lot to thank God for! But Christmas still looked bleak. It hurt not to be able to give our children presents!

'Tell me,' I asked them, 'why do you get presents for Christmas? Is it your birthday?'

Lynn, my serious, spiritual one, said, 'No. It's Jesus birthday.'

'Then why do people get the presents?'

The kids thought for a while and Lynn finally came up with the answer. 'Because we are remembering Jesus' birthday.'

'You're right. Jesus is the greatest Gift of all. He was God's present to the world.' I hesitated, then asked, 'What if you didn't get presents this Christmas?'

'But we always get presents for Christmas!' Renee wailed.

I let it drop. I just didn't have the heart to tell them there would be no gifts this year.

At this time Bob was driving along and saw a man who had been selling Christmas trees on a corner throwing away dozens of beautiful trees. Bob walked over and asked why he was throwing away the trees.

The man shrugged. 'It's two days before Christmas. Everyone has their tree now, so I decided to toss them.'

'Could I have them?' Bob asked hopefully. the man shrugged. 'Sure, I don't care.'

Bob stood up the trees again and set up shop. By nighttime he had sold every tree, except one, which he brought home and we decorated it together. Then to our wondering eyes, he brought in an armload of presents! God understands the heart of a child and he had planned all along that he would surprise them with Christmas presents.

On Christmas Eve, just like always, we read aloud the story of Jesus' birth from the 2nd chapter of Luke. And on Christmas morning we watched with joy as our children opened packages of dolls, games, clothing and a baseball glove for Stephen.

But we would always remember that it was Jesus' birthday, not ours, and that he was the greatest Gift of all!

Thanks be to God for his unspeakable Gift. 2 Corinthians 9:15.

Mrs Messing's Mailbox

When our daughters Lynn and Renee were ten and six years old, we lived in the rolling Tucson foothills. It was beautiful country, with a background of mountains and cactus, including the tall, stately saguaros. No longer in the old tin shed - God had now blessed us with a beautiful home with a swimming pool.

Our children had to walk a mile through the country to catch a school bus into the city but they didn't mind that too much. However, on one warm spring morning the girls started out. It was just too nice to spend a day at school.

'We could play hooky,' Lynn suggested with a sly grin. 'We could spend the day hiding in the desert and no one would even know.'

'Why don't we!' Renee quickly agreed. 'We have our lunches. Sure, it'll be fun!'

It was fun. At first. Hiding in a dry sandy streambed, they entertained themselves by watching the playful chipmunks and the leaping, bounding Jack rabbits. Once they saw a shaggy grey coyote slinking through the cactus and they sat very still, following it with their eyes. Soon, however, they tired of these things.

'It's kind of boring,' Lynn grumbled. 'School won't be out for a long time.'

'Let's walk for a while,' Renee suggested.

The road was empty of traffic, so they ambled along, finally coming to a mailbox.

Idly, Lynn opened the lid and peered inside. Wow! There were lots of letters! Giving Renee a daring look, Lynn scooped up the mail and closed the lid. Guiltily they scurried back into the warm hills to explore the letters.

'Oh look, Lynn!' Renee cried after peeling the envelope from one letter. 'Pictures!'

At the sound of a car stopping they quickly hid their sinful act in the sand. A familiar voice called, 'Okay, girls, I know you're there!'

'It's Mom!' Lynn hissed in terror.

Then she was coming toward them and there lay the shredded letters beside them.

'Mom,' Renee began in a small voice, 'we just didn't feel like going to school today.' (She knew the school had reported them missing.)

I got my girls in the car and we prayed together. Renee and Lynn looked a lot better after that – until I pulled up in front of Mrs Messing's home.

'What are you gong to do?' Renee squeaked.

'You're going to give Mrs Messing back her mail and tell her what you did. Mrs Messing is kind and loving and I'm sure she'll forgive you just like Jesus did.'

Mrs Messing came to the door and gave us puzzled looks. Looking like a sheep-killing dog, Lynn hung her head and held out the mail.

'I'm sorry we stole your mail, Mrs Messing. I don't know why we did it.'

Frowning, Mrs Messing took the mail. Instead of being angry, she spoke kindly to my daughters. Then she said an amazing thing. 'Why don't you girls come over on Saturday and we'll make cookies together?'

'You – you're not mad at us?' Lynn asked meekly.

'You did something wrong, but you've confessed and made it right. How about us starting over and being friends?'

True to her word, my girls went to Mrs Messing's house that very Saturday and came home with glowing reports of their good time together.

It's always important to confess our sins to Jesus, then make things right with the person we have hurt. Mrs Messing wasn't a Christian but we all learned a valuable lesson from her that day. Jesus wanted us to do that.

If we confess our sins, he is faithful and just to forgive us our sins, and to cleanse us from all unrighteousness. 1 John 1:9

That's what God did for my girls.

But I say unto you, love your enemies, bless them that curse you, do good to them that hate you, and pray for them which despitefully (wrongfully) use you and persecute you. Matthew 5:44.

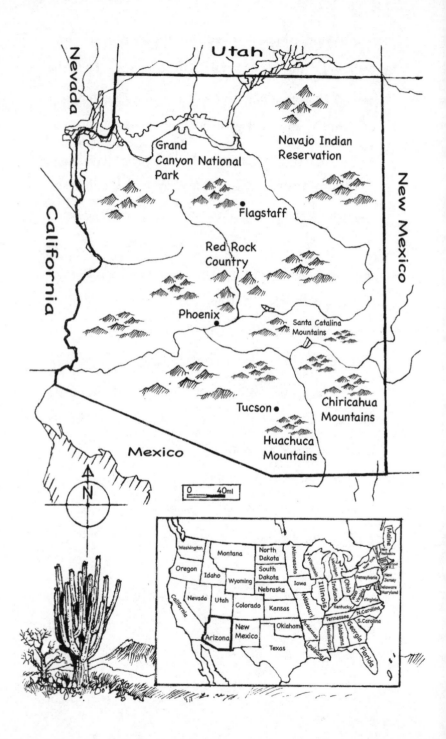

Author Information

Betty Swinford had been interested in writing since she was a little girl growing up in a small farming community in Indiana. She began to write when she was only eight years old by using an old toy typewriter. When she was eighteen years old she gave her heart to the Lord Jesus Christ and after that spent over thirty years in evangelistic work.

Betty spent most of her time writing books and teaching an adult Sunday school class. She had three children. One daughter, Lynn, is now with the Lord Jesus in heaven. Betty died in 2007.

As she lived right in the mountains of northern Arizona there was plenty of snow, a monsoon season, mountain lions and bears walking down the streets. The inspiration for this book came from her own life and experiences in this wonderful part of America that she called her home.

Rocky Mountain Quiz

1. What mountains are nicknamed the Cardboard mountains?

2. What are the only two venomous lizards in the world?

3. In the Bible when was it that Peter began to sink?

4. Where do Jack rabbits have their babies?

5. What is unusual about Jack rabbits when they are born?

6. How is our nature different to God's?

7. What do you need to hunt deer legally in Arizona?

8. How did the mountain 'Old Baldy' get its name?

9. When you don't feel as though God is around - does that mean that he has left you?

10. What are enchiladas?

11. What was unusual about the flock of sheep the family spotted?

12. Who is called The Great Shepherd of the Sheep?

13. What deer live in the Chiricahua Mountains?

14. What kind of walnut trees grow in Arizona?

15. The name of God is compared to a building. The righteous can run to it for safety. What is it?

16. What other country borders with Arizona?

17. What mountains are near the town of Patagonia?

18. Who gives instructions to protect you and who does he instruct?

19. What is another name for the mountains of Airzona?

20. What did George have to use to shear his sheep?

21. How does God want us to be like Lily the Sheep?

22. What kind of snake did Bob and Betty think they'd discovered?

23. What kind of snake did they actually discover?

24. What animal killed the foolish prophet in 1 Kings 13?

25. What kind of stone is Oak Creek Canyon made from?

26. In 1 Samuel 2:9 what part of the body is mentioned?

27. What does 1 Samuel 2:9 mean?

28. What is the name of the eight sided house that the Najajo live in?

29. What kind of jewelry do the Navajo Indians make?

30. What things work for the good of those who love God?

31. What precious metal can be found in Caò del Oro?

32. What animal did Bob and Betty see crouched in a tree?

33. What does God supply us with according to Philippians 4:19?

34. How many different kinds of scorpions are there?

35. What cactus can save your life if you are in the desert and dying of thirst?

36. What cactus can feed you?

37. What do the Navajo Indians use the Mesquite tree for?

38. What does Colossians 1:16 tell us about creation?

39. Who is the greatest gift of all?

40. What does God tells us to do about our sins?

Answers to Rocky Mountain Quiz

1. Santa Catalina mountains.

2. The bearded lizard and the Gila Monster.

3. When he took his eyes off Jesus.

4. On open ground - not in burrows.

5. They are born with their eyes open.

6. We are sinners he is holy.

7. A deer tag.

8. It doesn't have any trees on its top.

9. No it doesn't. God is always with us. Sometimes though he tests our faith.

10. Tortillas rolled into a tube and stuffed with cheese, then covered with a rich red sauce.

11. It didn't have a shepherd.

12. Jesus Christ.

13. White tail deer.

14. Black Walnut trees.

15. A strong tower.

16. Mexico.

17. The Huachuca mountains.

18. God and his angels.

19. The High Country.

20. Old fashioned hand clippers.

21. He wants us to trust him.

22. A King snake.

23. A poisonous Coral snake.

24. A lion.

25. Red sandstone.

26. Feet.

27. God will protect his people.

28. Hogans.

29. Silver and turquoise.

30. All things.

31. Gold.

32. A Black Panther.

33. All your needs.

34. 1,300.

35. The Saguaro cactus.

36. The paddle cactus.

37. The bean pods are used to make flour.

38. God created all things in heaven and earth.

39. Jesus Christ. 2 Corinthians 9:15.

40. Confess them. 1 John 1:9.

The Adventures Series
An ideal series to collect

Have you ever wanted to visit the rainforest? Have you ever longed to sail down the Amazon river? Would you just love to go on Safari in Africa? Well these books can help you imagine that you are actually there.

Pioneer missionaries retell their amazing adventures and encounters with animals and nature. In the Amazon you will discover tree frogs, piranha fish and electric eels. In the Rainforest you will be amazed at the armadillo and the toucan. In the blistering heat of the African Savannah you will come across lions and elephants and hyenas. And you will discover how God is at work in these amazing environments.

Scottish Highland Adventures by Catherine Mackenzie
ISBN 978-1-84550-281-2

African Adventures by Dick Anderson
ISBN 978-1-85792-807-5

Amazon Adventures by Horace Banner
ISBN 978-1-85792-440-4

Cambodian Adventures by Donna Vann
ISBN 978-1-84550-474-8

Great Barrier Reef Adventures by Jim Cromarty
ISBN 978-1-84550-068-9

Himalayan Adventures by Penny Reeve
ISBN 978-1-84550-080-1

Kiwi Adventures by Bartha Hill
ISBN 978-1-84550-282-9

New York City Adventures by Donna Vann
ISBN 978-1-84550-546-2

Outback Adventures by Jim Cromarty
ISBN 978-1-85792-974-4

Pacific Adventures by Jim Cromarty
ISBN 978-1-84550-475-5

Rainforest Adventures by Horace Banner
ISBN 978-1-85792-627-9

Rocky Mountain Adventures by Betty Swinford
ISBN 978-1-85792-962-1

Scottish Highland Adventures by
Catherine Mackenzie
ISBN 978-1-84550-281-2

Wild West Adventures by Donna Vann
ISBN 978-1-84550-065-8

TRAILBLAZER SERIES

Gladys Aylward, No Mountain too High
ISBN 978-1-85792-594-4

Corrie ten Boom, The Watchmaker's Daughter
ISBN 978-1-85792-116-8

Bill Bright, Dare to be Different
ISBN 978-1-85792-945-4

John Bunyan, The Journey of a Pilgrim
ISBN 978-1-84550-031-3

Amy Carmichael, Rescuer by Night
ISBN 978-1-85792-946-1

John Calvin, After Darkness Light
ISBN 978-1-84550-084-9

Jonathan Edwards, America's Genius
ISBN 978-1-84550-329-1

Michael Faraday, Spiritual Dynamo
ISBN 978-1-84550-156-3

Billy Graham, Just Get Up Out Of Your Seat
ISBN 978-1-84550-095-5

Adoniram Judson, Danger on the Streets of Gold
ISBN 978-1-85792-660-6

Isobel Kuhn, Lights in Lisuland
ISBN 978-1-85792-610-1

C.S. Lewis, The Storyteller
ISBN 978-1-85792-487-9

Martyn Lloyd-Jones, From Wales to Westminster
ISBN 978-1-85792-349-0

George Müller, The Children's Champion
ISBN 978-1-85792-549-4

Robert Murray McCheyne, Life is an Adventure
ISBN 978-1-85792-947-8

John Newton, A Slave Set Free
ISBN 978-1-85792-834-1

John Paton, A South Sea Island Rescue
ISBN 978-1-85792-852-5

Helen Roseveare, On His Majesty's Service
ISBN 978-1-84550-259-1

Mary Slessor, Servant to the Slave
ISBN 978-1-85792-348-3

Charles Spurgeon, Prince of Preachers
ISBN 978-1-84550-155-6

Patricia St. John, The Story Behind the Stories
ISBN 978-1-84550-328-4

Joni Eareckson Tada, Swimming against the Tide
ISBN 978-1-85792-833-4

Hudson Taylor, An Adventure Begins
ISBN 978-1-85792-423-7

John Welch, The Man who couldn't be Stopped
ISBN 978-1-85792-928-7

William Wilberforce, The Freedom Fighter
ISBN 978-1-85792-371-1

Richard Wurmbrand, A Voice in the Dark
ISBN 978-1- 85792-298-1

CHRISTIAN FOCUS PUBLICATIONS

Christian Focus | Christian Heritage | CF4K | Mentor

Christian Focus Publications publishes books for adults and children under its four main imprints: Christian Focus, Christian Heritage, CF4K and Mentor. Our books reflect that God's word is reliable and Jesus is the way to know him, and live for ever with him.

Our children's publication list includes a Sunday school curriculum that covers pre-school to early teens; puzzle and activity books. We also publish personal and family devotional titles, biographies and inspirational stories that children will love.

If you are looking for quality Bible teaching for children then we have an excellent range of Bible story and age specific theological books.

From pre-school to teenage fiction, we have it covered!

Find us at our web page:
www.christianfocus.com

CF4•K
Because you're never
too young to know Jesus